THE
MONEY
FORMULA

CHANGE YOUR RELATIONSHIP WITH MONEY
IN SEVEN STEPS & FIFTEEN MINUTES OR LESS

Leslie Juvin-Acker

WSA

PUBLISHING

Published by
WSA Publishing
301 E 57th Street, 4th fl
New York, NY 10022

Manufactured in the United States of America, or in the United Kingdom when distributed elsewhere.

Juvin-Acker, Leslie
        The Money Formula: Change Your Relationship to
        Money in 7 Steps & 15 Minutes or Less
        LCCN: 2018956102
        ISBN: 978-1-948181-23-5
        eBook: 978-1-948181-24-2

Cover design: Josh and Kayla Simpson
Cover photo by: Justin Nunez
Interior design: Claudia Volkman

http://themoneyformula.leslieinc.org

For Franck: Thanks to you, we cracked the code

Love, Leslie

TABLE OF CONTENTS

FOREWORD

I never thought that I would dictate a book from the source of all money: God.

I'll be honest—none of these ideas are my own. I just lean my ear into the wind and write down everything I hear. Pretty crazy way to write a book, huh? But many of the greats have done it. The struggle, strain, and drama of writing a book is just for show. In fact, it's very easy once you get the right idea. And an idea is just a thought that leads you on a train of consistent thought that creates a pattern. That's all.

If you would just quiet your mind to hear the whispers of the wind, your life would be a whole lot easier.

—Leslie Juvin-Acker

INTRODUCTION

I remember the moment. I was ten years old, and my parents had just moved us into our first real home (without wheels) on a dead-end dirt road called Solomon Street in Orange Park, Florida. It's a bedroom community on the outskirts of the military and logistics city of Jacksonville.

The grass was always soggy. The property was built on what could otherwise be called a bog. In fact, we couldn't be choosy as to where it was located because our home was gifted to us at an affordable rate by the Habitat for Humanity organization. For just $40,000, our family could afford to have a home. That's the kind of dignity this organization is all about; a hand up, not a handout.

You see, I'm the ambitious firstborn child of four of two unlikely lovers who met on the fringes of Clark Air Force Base, Philippines, in the early 1980s. I never thought I'd end up writing this book. Although at the age of ten, in that soggy backyard, I do remember having the exact thought that I would do two very important things.

First, I wanted to figure out why my dad struggled so

desperately to find and keep a job. He always seemed so unhappy when it came to his work. It was a constant source of pain and suffering for my parents. So much so that their fights were brutal, consistent, and never came to a resolution. I just wanted that to end, and I wanted to figure a way out. If not for him, for other people so their kids didn't have to feel the way I felt so often.

Second, I thought I'd do that by writing a book. The thought just came into my head like a flicker of a light bulb. And from that moment, I was obsessed with answering this question and, more importantly, solving it in a way that could be easily communicated to you.

So let's go on with the show!

ONE: MY STORY

My story actually begins before I was born. It started with my parents. Theirs was an unlikely love story between two young adults—too young by many standards. They were twenty and twenty-one when they began their life together. And each of them brought significant baggage into the relationship.

My dad was a small-town boy who grew up in Castle Rock, Washington. His parents were working-class professionals who met when they were fifteen and sixteen and were inseparable ever since. Their highest educational background was a General Equivalency Diploma (GED). Grandpa worked for the United States Postal Service and Grandma worked at the public school. They were both janitors. They built their own home on two acres at the base of the evergreen foothills of Mount St. Helens. Their life was meager, but it was dignified. Their parents came from humble origins. Both sides of the family immigrated from Scotland.

Grandpa's dad was an alcoholic and abused his only

1

son and wife. While Grandpa didn't beat his children, they were subjected to regular diatribes of criticism. And, no doubt, this went on to affect the self-esteem of Dad and his siblings.

My mom's parents were survivors of World War II. Their parents passed during the war. The children dispersed by marrying sailors and military men as a means to survive the decimation of the Philippines after the Japanese occupation. Grandma, who I call Lola, raised seven children in a world of unimaginable third-world poverty. And Grandpa couldn't hold a job, so he turned to the bottle and cigarettes. He was debilitated by a stroke which left him lame and unable to work.

To make ends meet, Lola's daughters were faced with two choices: marry an American G.I. or be forced into prostitution. Two of my aunts escaped the latter by marrying sailors, but my mom was not so fortunate. At fifteen, she was told to visit the local nightclub to dance for G.I.s, which meant on going on "dates" arranged by the club. Needless to say, my parents did not meet in a grocery store as they claimed when I was a small child.

Sexuality was always taboo in our family for this very good reason. But abuse was par for the course. Two young adults who were raised in an environment of abuse lacked the self-awareness and the self-esteem to build a healthy marriage, but they did their best to be parents.

I am grateful to say that I was not a point of focus in my parents' abusive marriage, but I was the principal witness.

MY STORY

Like a passerby at the scene of a crime, with morbid curiosity and fear of what would happen next if I didn't watch the violence, I saw my parents berate each other and beat each other senseless.

I developed severe anxiety as a child. The thought of going home where my father would be sleeping filled me with dread. I found every excuse not to go home, not to wake up the giant who would fill the house with terror.

And while I was avoiding his wrath, I saw my mom stand many nights at the kitchen sink helpless, alone, and sobbing; mumbling to herself in a half prayer, half confession for the struggles of her life.

As a child, you love your parents unconditionally. You want them to be happy so that your family can be happy. My parents' happiness became a condition for me to be happy. But that model of life is not self-sustaining, and I had to find my own happiness if I were to survive.

For much of my life, my story was not my story. It belonged to my parents'—and you'll soon learn how much of your story is *your* parents' too.

Through the process of discovering this essential fact, I have come to terms with the abuse that took place in our home. And as a result, I have found a deep sense of appreciation and gratitude for my parents, because what they went through wasn't easy. They took the hard way in so many ways for me, but they certainly didn't have to.

Here's why: life isn't meant to be a struggle. It's meant to be a journey of self-realization. It's meant to be a course on creativity, using the creative forces of life in the spirit of love and kindness. But too often we hold on to outmoded thinking long after the appropriate situation has passed, and we can't seem to figure out why the old ways of surviving no longer fit this new world we're living in.

Times change because we change. And in order to change in an easy way, we have to recognize that change is afoot and adjust ourselves accordingly. We are afraid of change because we've been conditioned to believe that change is hard, and painful, and full of suffering. So we avoid it, run from it, and deny it. But we can't avoid our prime directive to grow and change. We can't make the world stop spinning because we can't face a new day; this motion has been set into play long before any of us were even born.

So, with that said, embrace change. I believe that's why you're here today—you want serious, life-altering change. But you're stuck, and you don't know how to get unstuck. You're tired of leaving all the responsibility to Chance, and you're sick of watching the world pass you by. You're ready for a new life, but more importantly, what you're really ready for is *a new you*.

To see my childhood photos, log in to
The Money Formula Academy Dashboard:
http://themoneyformula.leslieinc.org

TWO: YOUR STORY AND A WARNING

Your story, like mine, begins before you were born. You chose your parents for a very important reason. And laced within them and the fragments of their lives are the things you're going to learn.

Your parents and their parents are co-creators of their reality. That is, everyone is creating their illusion of reality and are make-believing with others. That's right! Life is a big game of pretend! We find other people to act out scenarios and feelings so we can experience what it feels like.

Some people are conscious of this play. Like Shakespeare who said, "All the world's a stage, and all the men and women merely players." Others—for instance, those who jumped off buildings when their stocks crashed in 1929—not so much.

In no way am I being flippant about the true tragedies that happen across the world today— starvation, terrorism, abuse, and war. In fact, all of these things are make-believe that got out of hand. These involve a group of people who bought into a belief and were willing to commit gross atrocities in its name.

It was the French philosopher Voltaire who said, "Those who can make you believe absurdities can make you commit atrocities." And by golly, he was right.

I'm not willing to die for my beliefs. In fact, most of them are false. However, I will lay my head down for the truth. Because, in truth exists the wisdom that nothing is worth dying for—only worth living for!

I'm going to challenge everything you believe. I'm going to challenge your story. I'm going to show you my beliefs and my stories that led to years of total and complete fabrication!

So let this be my warning: The Money Formula is going to challenge every single belief you have about the following: yourself, the world, your parents, your attitudes, and your beliefs about the reason why you're here reading this book: money!

Remember, everyone is the hero in their own story. You'll come to learn how many villains you've created along the way. Consequently, you'll also find out that those villains are figments of your imagination.

The upside is that through this process of unwinding every story you've ever told yourself about money, your self-worth, and your life, you will come to meet the powerful creator that you are! How wonderful!

Don't worry. You're not alone in this experience. I've had clients who have felt rage, regret, and general confusion after experiencing The Money Formula. Here's why:

YOUR STORY AND A WARNING

You're going to feel angry at yourself for keeping money and financial abundance away from yourself for so long. You're going to want to kick yourself in the pants for the years wasted on financial struggle, arguing with your loved ones about money, and generally just feeling bad every time you thought of money. You will learn that you could have had it easy the entire time—and would have been left richer for it! Phooey!

You also may feel sad that you've missed opportunities. You may have said no to the joy of parenting children because you believed you weren't wealthy enough to raise them. You may have turned down an investment opportunity that could have left you a millionaire today. Or you could just be sad because you wasted so much of your life worrying about money instead of focusing on the things you love and that make you happy. You will learn that you could have had both this entire time—that you never had to make a decision between being rich and being happy.

Finally, you'll feel confused because I will shake up your entire belief ecosystem. I will wipe away the cobwebs in your mind so you can begin to see the world in a completely different way. And you may not know what to do with this new world! In fact, you might feel overwhelmed by the clarity and the wonder of having a fresh start.

Indeed, these are big claims, but I'm not joking. You're going to go on an emotional, mental, and spiritual roller coaster ride that may leave you exhausted. The good kind of exhausted—the way a marathon runner has rubbery legs at the end of a race. You will have accomplished something big with your life, but in subtle, powerful ways.

Let's start!

THREE: THE ORIGIN OF THE MONEY FORMULA

Franck and I are a real team. We've been that way from the start. But things didn't force us to *be* a team until he was laid off from his middle-management job at a international pool cleaner manufacturer in Vista, California. Until then, he was high on life living the American dream. A Frenchman who had dreamt of California since he was a boy, all he wanted to do was surf. His dreams came crashing down, however, in the wake of the 2008 global financial crisis.

He found himself unemployed just when he was about to marry the girl of his dreams (me), and he faced the harsh realities that so many Americans face each day: financial struggle. He was despondent. The day he was fired, he was so ashamed that he sat in his Honda Element outside of our Point Loma apartment for a good hour. From that moment, our financial lives were forever entwined. It forced us to put our heads together and talk about our careers, money, and what we wanted to do with our lives.

It was during that challenging life period that I evolved into a career coach. Franck is my number one client. I helped him pull his wounded ego out of the wreckage of his career and turn it into the career of his dreams. I took on this task for him, and I've helped countless other professionals do the same, too—to go on and make thousands, if not millions, of dollars more!

But there was one problem: no matter how many clients I had each month (some months over thirty), I could *never* make more than my husband. I could easily help him make $80,000 in one fell swoop—but me? Nope. Wasn't happening.

I was so embarrassed. It was my dirty little secret. I could help my clients negotiate record amounts of money. In fact, those clients who worked with me during the recession now make over 30 percent more than their peers in the exact same position. I could help others make money, but I couldn't help myself.

I kept going around in circles, trying to figure out why I couldn't pass the income threshold. I was hustling. I was marketing myself. I had a steady stream of clients. On paper, I did everything right. But there was something fundamentally wrong . . .

In the years after I recovered from postpartum depression and anxiety, I learned healing modalities as a way to help myself through the darkness of depression. I learned hypnosis, Emotional Freedom Technique, Neuro Linguistic Programming, Aroma Acupressure, and I even became a Reiki Master Teacher. I began to master my intuition and trust myself. I noticed how these techniques helped me, and I started using them with clients who were, like me, stuck on money.

My clients began reporting amazing results—such as eliminating hundreds and thousands of dollars of debt in days; getting new, better paying jobs in months; and finding money as though it were the road to Eldorado! And yet I still wasn't breaking past my own financial barriers.

I sat down and asked God to show me a better way, a faster way for clearing financial and emotional debt and limitations. And then this technique popped into my head and cleared a pathway for abundance like I had never seen before.

I sat down and followed the formula I'll share with you in this book. It works as a series of questions that reveal startling truths about a few things: your worldview, where you got this view, what your blocking belief is, and how you can replace that belief so you can totally change the way you feel about money.

Remember this from this point on: the word *money* feels differently to everybody. Just sit down with your friends the next time you're at dinner or having drinks and ask them to tell you the first thing they think of when you say "money." I guarantee the responses will all be different and revealing.

Download a Money Meaning Inventory Worksheet to find out your and others' financial word associations at The Money Formula Academy Dashboard: http://themoneyformula.leslieinc.org

Upon using The Money Formula for the first time, I realized how this *first thought* actually takes you right to the source of your limiting financial belief! Follow along with me . . .

When I thought about money, I immediately thought, *I'm not able to make as much as Franck.* I then began to feel a visceral response. I felt it in my stomach and chest. And I noticed that the feeling felt like guilt.

Next, going into that feeling, I asked myself, "When was the earliest critical moment I felt this way?"

Instantly I was transported to the kitchen in my parents' house on Solomon Street. I had this helpless feeling as a ten-year-old girl. My attention went immediately to the yellow spiral notepad hanging by the back door of the dining area. On it, my mom wrote out the family budget, all of the income and the expenses. She was very studious with money. Like me. She wrote everything down. Like me. She cut coupons. Like me. She had the survivor mentality of a Depression-era woman. Like me.

I remembered reading on that spiral notepad that my dad would make just enough to pay the bills. My mom always worked part-time jobs while we were at school or on Saturdays. She always made enough to cover the extras.

I decided to go deeper into the emotion of this memory, to an earlier age to get to the source of this feeling. I found myself at four years old, around the time my dad left the Air Force. He was an E3, and I remembered having this feeling that he could never get higher than this rank. I felt that he gave up. It was a helpless and hopeless feeling—a feeling I've felt many times when thinking about my own financial limitations.

Then it hit me like a ton of bricks. Two core beliefs jumped into my conscious mind:

- Dads/husbands make most, if not all, of the money.
- When you feel you've reached your max, you feel helpless, and you give up.

I slapped myself on the forehead. *Oh. My. God.*

Where did I learn this? My parents certainly did not consciously teach me to believe these ideas. I don't think my dad would have ever told my mom not to make more money than him. In fact, I'm sure he would have been happy for her and relieved for himself. Secondly, although my dad is not a wealthy man today, I'm sure he wouldn't ever have willfully wished his daughter to limit herself and her earning potential.

In this moment of dumbfounding realization, I instantly had flashbacks to all of the times in my life when I acted out these absurd beliefs. I BELIEVED that dads make all or most of the money, so when I told my husband to get a raise, the pure belief that I held within myself made that happen.

I only reached certain financial goals with my business when my husband set that goal for me. He would say,

"Okay, Leslie, we're going to need this much this month." And lo and behold, I would always match that goal—even if it caused me great discomfort. Because I BELIEVED that my husband set the tone for my financial success, I went along willingly with his commands—because that's exactly what my mother faithfully did.

And, to make matters worse, until the moment I discovered The Money Formula, I never made more money in a month than my dad because it was the only frame of reference I had. Everytime I thought money, I felt the guilt and saw that wirebound notepad hanging on the door—and what was on it? MY SALARY LIMIT!

Oh God, I thought to myself, *what am I going to do?*

Then I looked at my notes.

I realized that to stop the feeling, I had to go back to the thought, and to stop the thought, I had to break the pattern. I realized in that moment that in order to break the autopilot chain of behavioral habit, I needed to neutralize the emotional feeling to stop automatically returning to my financial frame of reference.

For my entire life and adult career, I had set my financial limit to what I saw on a piece of paper over twenty-two years ago. I was reeling. How could I possibly have gone on this long? I had a college education, along with additional expertise that would give me an honorary PhD somewhere; I had got years of proven success. Where did I go wrong?

Remember when I said earlier that children love their parents unconditionally? Well, when we love unconditionally, we trust unconditionally, and because children only pattern themselves after what they see and experience, we believe unconditionally. It's amazing that, as adults, we're so difficult to convince. Take a look at the political sides we have these days. That should be enough to remind you how stubborn adults can be. But children? No. They're flexible and malleable. Monkey see—monkey do.

Fortunately, we eventually begin to have a mind of our own. Our minds begin to rebel, and we start to question and debate everything our parents do. This program within the young mind helps to debunk the limiting beliefs of our parents. My dad knew better than to beat and verbally abuse his small children. He was fully aware of the pain abuse had caused him and he didn't want to do that to us. However, he wasn't aware of the insidious, crippling financial beliefs that he had learned along the way. In his reality, struggling financially was normal and socially acceptable—because everyone around him struggled. Why shouldn't he?

Don't get me wrong. I saw my dad try different get-rich schemes. He left us to try his luck in Las Vegas with my Uncle Pat, who became a drifter, a homeless man, and eventually a ward of the State of Washington. My dad traded eggs on the internet. He created a website called StopbyAgain.com with different links under different categories. This was about the time that I told him to buy freshly minted Google stocks; needless to say, he missed that boat.

There was a part of my parents that instinctively knew financial misfortune and working poverty wasn't natural.

But because everyone around them struggled, they didn't believe that there was a way out of the rat race. Not for one moment did they sit and say, "Hmm . . . I wonder why I feel this way every time I think about money?" They never bothered to ask, "Why do I suddenly start endless fights with my wife when we talk about money?"

Most people believe that fighting about money within the marital construct is normal. Boy, nothing could be further from the truth. Marriage is supposed to be a fun, co-creative space. But so many of us turn marriage into an institution of bad habits and poor financial hygiene.

Review your parent or caretaker's financial habits in The Family Money History worksheet on The Money Formula Academy Dashboard http://themoneyformula.leslieinc.org

But my Money Formula story didn't end there . . .

I shifted my mind again to the frustration surrounding money I experienced with Franck. We didn't constantly fight about money. We weren't mean to each other about it. But whenever we talked about money, I turned into the money manager and he turned into the incompetent, helpless fool. And when we went shopping, I could always feel his stress about spending. It was unbearable, and I modified my shopping behavior so I would rarely go shopping with him.

For the sake of our marriage, I couldn't let this dull, aching frustration continue any longer. It pained me to see my husband, who previously earned a six-figure income, live paycheck to paycheck. I found myself creating separate bank and investment accounts and stashing money away from him. This didn't align with my values, though, and I made the choice to stop the behavior.

I reapplied The Money Formula once more. I asked myself to think about Franck and money together. I felt the disgruntled frustration associated with this mental picture—that if I did something productive, his negative attitude would knock us off track. Then I noticed that I would spiral into negative financial thinking, accepting that our entire marriage would be this way.

I went into that disgruntled frustration and followed the feeling to the earliest memory. I remember that, when I was two years old, my mom accepted that she would manage the money and my dad would make it. I remembered that when I was around twelve years old, my mom would hide money from my dad so he wouldn't spend it when he got in a generous mood.

With further analysis of the events and the roles that each parent played in the relationship, another startling truth revealed itself to me: "Moms are responsible with money, and dads are irresponsible with money." This was what I believed!

I believed it so much that subconsciously I mimicked my mother's patterns. Hide money, create separate bank accounts, chastise Franck about his financial attitude, be the "bad guy."

I *believed* that all husbands were this way, especially mine. I judged without proof. I judged and *looked* for the proof—and when I relived the memories, there was no sufficient data to actually prove that my husband had ever been reckless or financially irresponsible. I created a reality with my belief and transferred it to my poor husband.

I was beside myself. It was time to come clean to Franck. I was so eager to tell him about what I had learned about this major limiting belief that I ran to his truck as soon as he came home from work. We stood in our cul-de-sac as I told him the story and apologized for the way I went about our marriage.

He was stunned, but then a sigh of relief rolled over him, and then a smile. He thanked me for finally acknowledging that I completely fabricated this false persona of him in a way to protect myself the way my mother had learned to protect herself. I was anticipating some kind of fallout that never happened, and instead I caused financial strife within my marriage. What a joke!

Download The Financial Roles Worksheet to see which financial roles replay themselves in your life at The Money Formula Academy Dashboard: http://themoneyformula.leslieinc.org

Dive Deep into the Matrix and Get Yourself Out

This all sounds absurd. "Of course, children mimic their parents!" a cynic might say. But this goes even deeper than just copying your parents' or caretakers' behaviors; it goes to a subconscious level so deep that you're not even aware you're doing these behaviors.

Just like in the film *The Matrix*, you think your experience is a result of someone else's thinking and doing. But it's really just an illusion you've created for yourself because you don't know any other way to live. You've got a DVD stuck in the player that you've put on repeat. You're not even aware that you can take it out and watch the other films in your library. This is how deep the rabbit hole of a lack of an awareness is that you're in.

That's what we struggle within in life: a lack of awareness. When we become aware of this "lack" of awareness, we translate that to a general sense of lack in our lives. And then we see lack everywhere, and we apply it to money and abundance. It overwhelms and burdens us, but it doesn't have to.

You see, there is no such thing as "lack"—it's an illusion. You lack absolutely nothing. And everything you have is the maximum capacity of your present imagination. The more you expand your imagination and your awareness of what is possible, the more you can experience and have in life.

The Money Formula seeks to break this powerful illusion. By the end of this book, you're going to stop seeing lack in your life. You're going to know, for sure, that there is no such thing as lack. Like Amazonians in the rainforest, you're going to be surrounded by everything you need and more. You're not going to be concerned with what is across the sea in a city you've never been to that has something you supposedly "need." You're going to believe and know that what you need to get to the next step of abundance is immediately within and around you. How liberating!

Once I realized these essential false beliefs, I was able to attain new facts and a new framework for living. This is what I learned:

- I can make as much, if not more than my husband.

- I can attract an unlimited amount of money in a month, a day, and even an hour.

- Not all husbands/dads are financially irresponsible. My husband is as financially responsible and level-headed as they come.

- I don't have to be the financial "heavy" in the family. I can be my normal, happy, carefree self.

- I can feel proud and happy with all the money I bring, no matter how much.

These facts translated themselves into new beliefs. And, as a result, they completely neutralized the immediate negative thought that came with the words money and husband+money. Since I no longer immediately think a negative thought when these words come up, I am now free to choose and even reset the protocol that inspires my next choices and behaviors.

By taking away the trigger of that first thought and neutralizing my feelings surrounding money, I become powerfully aware of the causative factors that influenced my behavior. And, since the electricity charge isn't there to set me on a death spiral of negativity, I don't do those behaviors anymore. I don't argue with my husband (I can disagree, but we don't fight). I don't hide money. And I certainly don't see limits for myself any longer. It's liberating to not have to go on an automatic tailspin of the same old thoughts about money. Instead I find myself spiraling up to new levels of imagination, and I'm no longer afraid to take calculated risks when it comes to my business and finances.

Now that you understand the general premise of The Money Formula, I'm going to take you through some case studies that verify this formula. Surprisingly, within the first week, I tested The Money Formula on several friends and clients—and it all worked . . . and in less than fifteen minutes!

The Money Formula is easy to do, takes very little time, and offers a powerful punch. Learn more about limiting beliefs from these case studies and see if you recognize any of your own.

Are you ready? Let's go!

To see a follow up conversation with me and Franck, log into The Money Formula Academy at http://themoneyformula.leslieinc.org

FOUR: ALBERT'S MONEY FORMULA

Albert is a happily married man and a successful engineer. By all accounts, he has his finances in order with plenty of cash to spare. He was curious as to how he may have been self-sabotaging his financial life.

In a session, he and his wife sat down with me. Albert did all of the talking, but he felt self-conscious with his responses because he did not want to upset his wife with his honesty. I began to use The Money Formula with him, but he was analyzing his answers instead of going to the first, immediate place in his mind.

When I assured him that giving the most spontaneous, honest answers he could give would help enhance his financial life and improve his marriage, he began to give direct responses.

Because I did not know his personal story, I couldn't determine what his Money Formula was until I saw the entire picture. You'll soon learn what I discovered in that session.

When I asked Albert to give me his first immediate thought of money, he said he saw his parent's home with a tennis court on the property.

Then I asked him to give me his first immediate feeling when he thought of money. He said, "A conflicted feeling between being out of control and knowing that money is irrelevant in the grand scheme of life."

Next I asked him to go to the earliest memory he could remember when he felt this way.

Immediately he told me what happened when he was just four years old. He said:

> I remember being in my dad's antique sports car. I'm sure he told me not to touch anything, but as soon as he turned around and went to go get something, I put the car out of gear, from park to neutral. Suddenly I was rolling down the driveway completely out of control. Fortunately, my dad managed to stop the car in time. In that moment, I felt afraid that I was going to get in trouble for having some fun.

I asked him what role his dad played in that moment. He said, "The protector." Then I asked him what he was trying to do by moving the gears. He answered, "I was just having fun, and suddenly it felt chaotic."

Next I asked him to draw the parallels in his financial life. I said, "Who now in your adult life plays the little boy and who plays the role of your dad, the protector?"

Without hesitation, he said, "Oh, my wife plays the role of the dad!"

His wife nodded in agreement and said, "Whenever he

wants to buy a toy or have some fun, he emails me asking me for permission. But it stresses me out because I have to be the bad guy to keep our family (financially) safe."

Albert agreed with this assessment and added, "But you have to admit that this strategy keeps our family financially afloat."

"It works?" I asked the couple.

"Yes," said Albert's wife, "but I don't want to be that person anymore. It's too stressful for me."

As you can see, Albert had recreated his childhood situation. He was the little boy having fun, and his wife was his dad reeling him in, just in time before major damage or trouble happened. This couple played these roles despite the stress of Albert's wife and the unnecessary damage in their relationship. In this session, Albert's wife realized that she didn't have to be someone she's not—a stressful naysayer—to keep their family in a healthy financial place.

In order to reverse their money formula, Albert had to first realize that he was recreating an unnecessary relationship dynamic in his marriage. The couple no longer had to play fictional roles to stay afloat and thrive financially. Second, Albert didn't have to make the choice between having fun in life and being financially responsible. Third, Albert could take on the role as dad—he could make safe financial decisions for himself and not put unnecessary pressure on his wife to be the "responsible party." Yes, they could share in the decision, but she no longer had to be the "Negative Nancy" constantly reminding him of his priorities.

Within the context of this couple, it was clear that one of the biggest winners of The Money Formula is Albert's wife. The burden of financial responsibility no longer rests solely on her shoulders, and together the couple can come up decisions together instead of one approving the request of the other.

The temptation is there to accept the outdated Money Formula because "it works." But now that Albert and his wife are both aware of the dynamics and old roles, the less inclined they are to want to play them again. Albert's wife *knows*—not just believes—that she doesn't have to be the bad guy when it comes to money. Albert can't make her play that role anymore. She also knows that Albert is not her "financially irresponsible husband"; she can trust him to create fun with money and make smart, safe financial decisions at the same time. The illusion is broken— there is no going back!

In this powerful session, The Money Formula worked in less than fifteen minutes and forever transformed Albert's marriage and financial success. He and his wife no longer believe that they're the characters they initially thought they were, and so the story has completely changed. That's the beauty of The Money Formula!

To watch and listen to the updates about Albert and his wife, log into The Money Formula Academy at http://themoneyformula.leslieinc.org

FIVE: SUSANNA'S MONEY FORMULA

Susanna was a single busy professional. If you didn't know it, from the outside you'd judge that she was a workaholic. She worked endless hours for her company as a sales manager, helping the company break through a one-million-dollar mark in record sales. But if you looked at her finances, Susanna was barely making ends meet. Her small salary left her feeling overwhelmed by work, and as a result she didn't have a personal life. It was no surprise that she burned out and came to me for help.

I asked Susanna to take me to her first thought when she thinks of the word *money*.

She answered, "Security and work."

I asked her what emotions are attached to security and work, and she said she felt a ball of emotions.

I then instructed her to go into those emotions and follow them to the earliest memory she could recall feeling this exact way. What came next completely revealed why she had struggled with her finances her entire professional career.

Susanna said that she was immediately taken to a moment when she was three years old. She was sitting in the kitchen one evening with her father, who was showing her how to eat Oreo cookies. In that moment, she asked her dad, "Where's Mama?"

He explained where she was and did his best to console her. Susanna said that she felt sadness that her mother had to work long nights in order to maintain security for the family. I asked her what she learned to believe about life in that moment. She said:

> I learned that if you want to be financially secure, you needed to work long nights. I have always felt this compulsion to work late that I could never explain. It made me feel heavy, and I worried that I was being a workaholic. I remember having to pull myself away from work, but not knowing why I couldn't just stop working so that I could enjoy my personal life.

But the realizations didn't stop there for Susanna.

> Now that I think of it, I have this memory of myself in college. I used to say over and over again, "I'd rather be poor and have time for my children or be super rich so that I don't need to work so I can focus on my kids, but nothing in between."

SUSANNA'S MONEY FORMULA

Susanna next revealed that she had had three miscarriages. She had written her Money Formula in such a way that it was impossible for her to have children. Since she was not in absolute poverty and wasn't filthy rich either, in her mind children had no place in this "in-between" reality she had created. Realizing that she had this role shocked her to her core.

Susanna felt a wave of grief and sadness. She said she felt so sad that she had closed the door on the opportunity of motherhood because of the belief system she created around money. She realized that she never had to make a choice between motherhood and financial security. In Susanna's old world, she played the role of the absentee mother. And, since she was consciously aware of how painful it was for her to have so few childhood memories with her own mother, she "spared" her children this grief by not carrying them to full term.

Susanna felt strangely liberated by this truth. She realized that she didn't have to play the struggling woman who had to work late nights for little pay. Nor did she have to play the woman who couldn't have children because she wasn't there for them. She also realized that she no longer had to work without having fun.

Instead Susanna realized that she could get paid to have fun at work. She could have healthy business hours and be compensated generously for it. Her new Money Formula was Money = Fun. Additionally, Susanna learned the important truth that she didn't have to choose between a family and wealth through a profitable career. She could now have both!

It's true that The Money Formula will shake up everything you've ever known about money. In Susanna's case, she didn't realize that she had arbitrarily chosen between a family life and career in order to have money. This old Money Formula simply didn't work within the framework of reality.

You don't have to experience burnout to get to the point that Susanna did before changing your Money Formula. Susanna's financial beliefs set her free to find new ways of living, and I'm sure she's glad she did. Because who wants to live a life like Scrooge, alone and miserable?

Indeed, wealth and abundance are for sharing. A family is a wonderful opportunity to grow abundance. Unfortunately many people find that having a family is a source of financial stress because that's where they learned their limiting financial beliefs. Like my next story, for example.

To watch and listen to the updates about Susanna, log into The Money Formula Academy at http://themoneyformula.leslieinc.org

SIX: PETER'S MONEY FORMULA

Peter was a successful senior-level professional. He made over six figures, but he couldn't seem to break past living paycheck to paycheck. He always seemed to have just enough to get by. He also was stressed that he couldn't manage to get a pay raise even after having completed a successful project for his company. Not knowing what to do, he came to see me.

Peter was ready to make a change, but he didn't know how. He recently had asked for a raise and a promotion, but his CEO never even bothered to return his requests for a response. This is where I began to discover Peter's Money Formula.

I asked Peter what the first thought that came forward was when he thought of money. He said, "Not enough."

I said, "How do you feel when that thought comes up?"

He told me that he felt anger and guilt that mixed inside his abdomen, just above his appendix. I asked him to go to the earliest memory when he felt this way.

He took me back to when he was six years old. He remembered sitting alone in his childhood bedroom, staring out of the second-story window. He said that he felt sad and alone, stuck because he had nowhere to go. He said he had called some friends to see if he could play with them, but their parents said no. I asked him if his mother would play with him, and he said she was too busy to play with him because she was worried about everything else. He added that if he asked her to play or to buy him something to play with, she made him feel guilty for even asking.

What Peter learned in that memory was that he had to feel bad for asking for something that could make him happy. He said that when he called his friends, he would start every phone call with "I'm sorry for disturbing you . . ."; he went into every conversation already apologizing for asking for what he wanted. Rejection was a self-fulfilling prophecy.

Peter learned through this exercise that his financial situation perfectly imitated the role he played as a child—a regretful, guilty person feeling bad for even bothering to ask for something he desperately needed: happiness. Together Peter and I discovered that he equated money to approval that he'd never get. In her distraction, his mother unwittingly made him feel guilty for asking for something, and as a result, Peter felt guilty for asking for a raise and a promotion, even though he knew he deserved it.

In fact, Peter revealed, he felt guilty for even being alive. The guilt he felt for having needs made him feel that he had to survive on the bare minimum. He felt angry toward his mom for not appreciating him as a child and not valuing his place in the family as a source of happiness instead of financial stress. His initial thought of "not enough" really meant "I'm not enough for my mother."

Peter created a situation in which he had to ask for approval to get more money in his life. Then, if he didn't get that approval, he'd struggle along with just enough money to meet his basic needs, much to the strain of his health and family relationships. Peter was so worried about getting his CEO's approval that he felt guilty for asking for a well-deserved raise. Since he never got the approval, he never got more money. Because he didn't get either, he felt angry and resentful toward his CEO; he saw himself as a "good boy" who didn't get what he deserved from his "distracted" boss who didn't appreciate him.

As a father, Peter loves his children and sees their value in his life. Because he is mindful of their contribution to the happiness of the family, he is prepared to invest in them. Peter's Money Formula centered around family. His professional story was a repeat of how he felt as a child. When he wasn't aware of this dynamic and the roles he played, he continued the pattern and paid dearly for it with financial struggle.

To reverse his Money Formula, Peter learned that he didn't have to wait for anyone's approval to create financial abundance. In fact, he could approve of his financial increase with his belief alone. Because he no longer believed that he had to wait for his mother, his boss, or anyone else for an increase, he could begin to look for other financial opportunities and take his financial life back into his own hands. He didn't have to feel bad for asking for money, either. He could ask the Universe and know it would be granted to him posthaste. What a powerful affirmation that Life really wants us to be abundant!

As you can see, The Money Formula can reveal striking layers of dysfunctional financial beliefs. There is an eco-system of self-limiting beliefs that pervades your financial life and business relationships. It's no wonder that you can learn to blame others in your life for the fact that you are suffering financially. They may not even be aware of their impact on you, so it's vitally important to know that you can completely change your Money Formula even if others never realize their mistakes and their behaviors.

That's right. You can change your entire Money Formula even if your loved ones don't change. You can have abundance, keep abundance, and feel financially secure even if your loved one doesn't. What will change is your trust in yourself and in the Universe to provide your every need. You no longer have to believe that your financial success is in the hands of any other person in your life.

 *To watch and listen to the updates about Peter's story, log into The Money Formula Academy at http://themoneyformula.leslieinc.org*

SEVEN: TERRY'S MONEY FORMULA

Terry was struggling with money. He made over six figures, but he found himself in debt and in a strained relationship. While he was focusing on his work and his financial situation, he claimed his girlfriend (the mother of his child) was hounding him incessantly by saying that he didn't trust her. He struggled with neck and back pain as a result of the tension these life areas caused him. He was aggravated by her insecurity. Something had to change.

I began by asking him, "What is the very first thought you think when you think of money?"

He said, like Peter, "Not enough."

Next I asked him, "What are the very first feelings you feel when you think this thought?"

Terry said he felt pressure and stress. I asked him to recall the earliest memory when he felt this pressure, and he said it was when he was about ten years old and his parents divorced. He said he acutely remembered hearing his mom complain about his dad and how he took everything from her in the divorce. That's when he began to worry about finances.

Knowing that everyone's Money Formula begins between birth and age seven, I asked him to go deeper into
the worry he felt and to tell me what memory he associated with it.

Instantly the light bulb went off in his head. He knew the
source of his money pressure. He said:

> I remember when my mom and dad were still mar-
> ried, and I was seven years old. At the time, they
> were both having affairs—my mom with her golf
> buddy and my dad with another woman. I didn't
> know it at the time because they sheltered me, but
> I sensed great distrust between them. The core of
> the breakdown was that they had a lack of imag-
> ination in their relationship and a lack of compas-
> sion for each other.

From that emotional experience, Terry learned that he
couldn't trust his life partner, because that type of relationship was rampant with stress and judgment. As a result of
the fundamental belief he learned when he was a boy observing his parents, he created a reality in which his present relationship (and even earlier ones) were dragged into
dramas around cheating. His current girlfriend continually
accused him of cheating even though he had never cheat-
ed on her or any other woman.

Terry's belief that intimate relationships can't be trust-
ed colored his romantic relationships and caused him to

fear that relationships always end in breakup and financial loss. Terry's Money Formula made him believe that his relationship with money equals worry, accusations, and being one-sided. Furthermore he learned to equate money with dysfunctional relationships. Often Terry found himself arguing on the phone with creditors and service providers on the phone. This, too, was a figment of his imagination and a recreation of past events.

Terry discovered that he did not need to recreate his parent's relationship with each other and their relationship with money in order to experience financial trust and security. He also didn't need to blame his girlfriend for their dysfunctional relationship because he realized he was creating the dysfunction through his flawed perception of reality. He is not his mother, and his girlfriend is not his father.

In order to reverse his Money Formula and feel good about money, Terry needed to do some key things:

- Use his imagination to create new financial solutions
- Use empathy and compassion to understand each other's issues
- Foster an environment of trust and only do business with trustworthy individuals

I asked him what kind of emotional environment he was in when his business partnerships were the most successful. He said, "Trusting and compassionate."

I instructed Terry to create environments of trust and to build relationships around that trust. If he did, he would find more financial opportunities and greater ease and relaxation in those situations. He would no longer need to associate money with stress. Instead he could associate money with great relationships. Then to find money, he would only need to look for those great relationships. And to make more money, he could foster those relationships into healthy ones. Terry's secret to great success and wealth was simple: look for and build great relationships.

The reason it's so important to change the way you think about money is that our thinking about it has become habitual. The problem is that we've inherited someone else's habits and beliefs. We've twisted the reality of a traumatic situation so we could make sense of what we didn't understand. Then, instead of internalizing and processing that ignorance, we project it onto others needlessly and painfully.

Terry's story is quite common. We create scenarios over and over and wonder why they don't stop. We wonder why our relationships struggle, why money is hard to come by, and why we can't muster up more of it. We compartmentalize our personal life and our financial life, and we don't see the connection between the two.

Remember, we all have a relationship with money. If you want to see how someone is doing financially, look at their relationships. Are they transactional? Are they unhealthy? Are they looking for approval? These behaviors indicate some of the patterns and limiting beliefs we've picked up over the years. It's no surprise that those with poor relationship-building skills struggle with money.

You can have a lot of money and struggle in certain relationships. In fact, my clients who are multimillionaires and come see me during times of great financial struggle also are facing personal struggles of their own. Indeed, I worry about professionals if their relationships were transactional and shortsighted. It generally means that their financial strategy is not much different.

It's no surprise that our relationship with money is modeled after the key relationships we've had the most exposure to during our formative years. This next story of a dysfunctional relationship will demonstrate how our early relationships shape not only our relationship with money, but also our relationship with life.

To watch and listen to the updates about Terry, log into The Money Formula Academy at http://themoneyformula.leslieinc.org

EIGHT: ELAINE'S MONEY FORMULA

Elaine was struggling in her marriage. Her husband was verbally abusive, and she knew her constant complaining and negativity pushed him over the edge. She was looking for a way out of the unhealthy marriage and wanted someone to tell her that she didn't deserve his abuse, even though she was a self-professed complainer. She was also stuck in her career, but every time she came to see me about her career, she ended up talking about her husband instead.

When I asked her what her first thought was when she heard the word *husband*, she said, "Go away."

I then asked her to tell me what she felt when she thought that phrase, and she said she felt a dread and heaviness in her stomach and chest. She said the dread was characterized by feelings of loneliness, chaos, embarrassment, and confusion.

I told her to go back through that feeling to the earliest memory she could remember. We eventually went back through time to when she was ten years old and dreaded going to school in the morning. Going deeper and earlier into that time, she brought me back to a key memory when she was just four years old.

Elaine said that her mother regularly dropped her off with an abusive babysitter. Her mother did not know the babysitter was abusive, and since Elaine couldn't communicate the abuse, this went on for years. One particular day Elaine was frightened and wanted her mother to stay with her. She kicked and screamed, but her mother ignored her pleas.

Elaine felt angry that she couldn't communicate her needs to her mother, and she was equally angry at her mother for not having her life together. Because, she reasoned, if her mother had her own life together, she would never have to leave Elaine with the abusive babysitter in the first place. Elaine came to rely on this abusive babysitter and learned that the only way to get her mother's love and attention was to kick, scream, and complain even if only to be ignored after the display.

I asked Elaine what she learned from this life experience. What she said next was surprising.

Elaine said that people will never understand each other because a) they don't know what they want and how to communicate it; and b) people don't have the self-awareness to understand how another person feels.

With these two core beliefs, Elaine established the foundational experience for her marriage. On top of that, she created a marriage in which her husband, playing the role of her mother, ignored her needs *and* didn't have his life together.

ELAINE'S MONEY FORMULA

This was a very difficult reality for Elaine to accept. It was hard for her to see how these two situations were related, because as far as she was concerned, no matter what she thought and did, her husband would never change. I told her that this statement was evidence of her belief that no matter what she did, her financial experience would never change. She created a complex situation with simple underlying beliefs.

If you believe that no matter what you do, your financial situation will never change, then you are absolutely correct. Our beliefs create self-fulfilling prophecies. If you believe that no matter what you do, money will always follow you, then you are also correct. Belief goes both ways.

I then asked Elaine if life loved her unconditionally. She immediately said no. I asked her if she loved unconditionally. Her guilty-looking face gave me the response I needed to prove to her that because she was so conditional with her love toward her husband, her mother, and abuser, as a result, her version of life was conditional in its love toward her.

Elaine was able to see that she was distracting herself from advancing her career and finances by complaining about her husband. As far as she was concerned, she was making twice as much money with her job in half as many hours as her husband. In her relationship with money+husband, she felt self-righteous and felt that she had her life together, but he didn't, and so she had no reason to change. She believed he was the one who needed to change.

It's no surprise that Elaine's career didn't change. Even though she consciously wanted it to change because she was unhappy at her current job, she subconsciously programmed the belief into her mind that she had no reason to change.

As you can see, Elaine had many limiting beliefs surrounding money and relationships. We all do. What The Money Formula demonstrates to us is that we can reveal and unroot several limiting beliefs by applying it over and over as each triggering thought and feeling is revealed.

In order for Elaine to reverse her Money Formula, several key beliefs needed to change:

- She had to forgive herself for being unable to communicate her need for safety and love.
- She had to forgive her mother for not "having her life together" according to Elaine's standards.
- She needed to believe that life loves her unconditionally, and that she, too, is able to love others unconditionally—even those abusers that she attracted into her life.
- She needed to eliminate the belief that life wouldn't change no matter what she did.

With these fundamental beliefs eradicated, Elaine could finally own up to the fact that she was creating an unhappy marriage because she expected to be married to a person who was unable to communicate his needs and didn't have his life together. Her husband was held hostage by Elaine's belief that all marriages are abusive and dysfunctional. When Elaine could finally accept that her husband was not the person she created him to be, should could allow herself to love him unconditionally and believe that if she communicated her needs clearly, he'd be able to reciprocate.

I told Elaine that no matter what happened—whether she decided to stay married or get divorced—her being in a state of unconditional love would attract the ideal relationship with her husband. She also could finally move forward in her career and achieve the financial security she desired by letting go of the distraction of a dysfunctional and unequal marriage.

To watch and listen to the updates about Elaine and her husband, log into The Money Formula Academy at http://themoneyformula.leslieinc.org

NINE: LIVING THE CORE PRINCIPLES OF THE MONEY FORMULA

To master The Money Formula, there are a few key principles you must understand and apply. They are very simple and require only mental focus and application for them to work. There is nothing you need to do except to be totally and completely focused upon these principles when you think about them.

Principle Number 1: In Any Case You Can Imagine The Money Formula Working or Not Working, You Are Right

You have an acute ability to create exactly the reality you wish to experience. The moment you put your mind on a thought and make an immediate emotional connotation—either good or bad—you will then unleash a sequence of events that will fulfill your prophecy.

So, if you say that The Money Formula doesn't work for you, you're right! No guarantee in the world that I make to you will change this fundamental fact. As I mentioned earlier, YOU are the powerful creator of your experience and what you say goes in your reality. In the words of Henry Ford, "Whether you think you can or you think you can't, you're right."

Principle Number 2: Your Imagination Is the Secret to Your Wealth and Success

When I was five years old, my first consciously remembered inner dialogue was, "I need to use my imagination if I'm going to have fun here (in life)."

You can have every instrument of creativity available to you in life, such as musical instruments, art supplies, metalworking tools, and so forth, but if you don't have an ounce of imagination, curiosity, and focus, then none of these things will work for your amusement.

You see, money is merely a tool for your amusement. However, you don't use the tool because you don't have a purpose for it. Your imagination will create what you want out of life. Unfortunately we don't use our imaginations; instead we default to the protocols and beliefs we inherited from our parents and authority figures growing up. We default to societal norms and then find ourselves miserable, broke, and unhappy when we discover that those norms won't give us what we truly want to express. What a lazy and self-sabotaging way to live!

Which brings me to the next principle . . .

Principle Number 3: You Must Have a Clearly Defined Purpose for the Wealth You Intend to Acquire

You can have and do anything in life, it's true. However, without seeing a clearly defined purpose for that which you want to experience with your money, you simply won't have it. Here's why:

Everything you think comes to manifestation in one way or another. Many people say on occasion, "Boy, I sure would love to have a million dollars right about now!"

But what do they do next? They go on to watch reality TV shows, engage in dramas in the workplace or amongst their social circle, and they spend time complaining about the system and how unfair it is. Did I forget to mention that they complain about how much money they *don't* have?

You are consciously aware that being wealthy and rich are better than being poor and struggling, but you instantly default to negative thinking and behaviors the moment you think about money.

This is why the moment you think about money, it is critical to imagine what you'll do with it and the purpose of having it in your life. The Money Formula gets you to stop negative, self-sabotaging thinking about money and gets you to immediately go to where it will have purpose.

Nobody goes to the bank and says to the loan officer, "Hey, I'd like a bunch of money, please. I'll let you know what I'll do with it once I get my hands on the cold, hard cash."

They'd laugh you out of the building!

Instead, you must have a clearly thought-out strategy for this money: what you intend to do with it, how you will use it to increase its value, and how you intend to pay it back.

In the case of The Money Formula, your subconscious and conscious mind both need to know what you intend to do with your wealth—how you intend to grow it (for example, if you want a nicer car, where will you go and what will you do with it), and how you intend to pay it back (for example, how you will pay it forward with kindness and generosity, perhaps sharing your car with your family or give your friends rides to the airport).

The Universe and your subconscious mind have to work in harmony with purpose and imagination. When you believe that both will cooperate to help you achieve your vision of wealth and abundance, they will work together effortlessly on your behalf.

Principle Number 4: Visualization Is Key

A lot of people don't understand what visualization is. They make it more tricky than it actually is, but in fact it's quite simple. I'm sure you do it all of the time.

Imagine the last time you had a major financial conflict in your life. Maybe you faced a lawsuit, or a dispute over rent, or someone owed you money and you really needed it. What happened? What did you do?

LIVING THE CORE PRINCIPLES OF THE MONEY FORMULA

Odds are you thought nonstop about it in the car, while you were on your walks, while you were taking a shower and brushing your teeth, and even while you were wide awake at night. You visualized the person and what you would say if they said that. What they would say if you said this. You ran through every possible scenario until you prepared yourself for the conflict that was to come.

All of us have done this at one point or another. This is called *visualization*. You can call it *rehearsal* instead.

World-famous UFC mixed martial artist and boxer Conor McGregor rose to meteoric fame and success by saying this about the art of visualization:

> If you have a clear picture in your head that something is going to happen and a clear belief that it will happen no matter what, then nothing can stop it. It is destined to happen. It's perfect.

Every day rehearse your vision of financial success. Go from the conception of your very first idea—which is critical to The Money Formula—and follow that thought until it is fully realized. Give that thought purpose, give that thought a job, and follow the positive wave of emotion that this inspired idea brings you. Allow yourself to go on the treasure hunt this rehearsal process gives you.

Which leads me to the next principle: live in only one reality.

Principle Number 5: There Is One, Singular Universe if You Want to Be Rich

The beauty of being a human being is that we have the possibility of being two places at the same time—in our physical body and in the reality of our mind.

Have you ever been hanging out with someone and they are telling you about their day, but you didn't hear any of it because you were thinking about what you were going to have for dinner?

Everybody does this. This function helps us continue our path of creation. This is a faculty of the mind and imagination that helps us continue what we've started. And if we've created a reality we don't like—let's say we're stranded on the side of the road with a flat tire—we can imagine what resources are available to us while we're standing there. We can think back to the time we saw our dad fix the flat with a spare. Or we can remember that our auto insurance has roadside service. We can think our way out of any situation. It's that simple.

We can use this ability either as a detriment or as a life-changing skill. I remember how my dad would be in the same house as us, but his mind would usually be a million miles away. We never connected emotionally, and because of that distance, we're not close today.

However, if properly anchored to a constructive ideal, the use of your mind to harness alternate realities can bring you immense wealth and happiness.

Here's an example. One day, while my husband, Franck,

and I were driving along the 101 in Solana Beach, California, I was looking out the window. The kids were seated in the backseat and my husband was at the wheel. As I looked at the beautiful coastline on that gorgeous day, I had a vision—a sneak peak of things to come.

I saw that Franck and I would buy a house within the year. I felt at peace and confident that this would come to fruition. I just *knew* I was going to be a homeowner once again. However, there was one big stark reality: we had zero money to put down on a house.

I said to Franck, "Spirit (this is what I call my intuition) says that we're going to buy a house within a year!"

He looked at me in disbelief. Being the realist in the situation, he said, "I don't know how we're going to do that. We don't have any money."

I just *knew* that the money was going to come through, and somehow our dream house would come to us. All I said to Franck at that point was, "I don't need you to know how it's going to happen. All I need from you is to agree with me and just say yes."

And so he chuckled to himself and said, "Okay. Yes!" That was the end of the conversation.

Within eight months, we received just under $100,000 as an unexpected gift through an inheritance. It was the exact amount we needed to put down a down payment and cover closing costs and taxes. We also could do some minor renovations to get the house set up for my new office and build a fence for the kids.

To double down on this miraculous visualization story, when I was about eight years old, I imagined that I had a large amount of money waiting for me in a Swiss bank account. The money we received for the house originated from a long lost family member of Franck's who detested his family so much that he hid millions of Euros in a Swiss bank account. Franck's grandmother inherited part of this large sum as a result, and some of the money was eventually passed down to Franck.

When you visualize, imagine that this is the only reality in which you are living. If, in your imagination, you are a multimillionaire, live as though you are. You don't have to know how it will materialize, but you have to believe that being a multimillionaire is true and possible for you. If you are a prize fighter like Conor McGregor, do everything that a champion boxer does. Eat everything a champion boxer eats. This is your only reality, so you have to make every moment count.

Use your imagination sparingly. This is a warning to those who like to get caught up in stories. The case studies in this book show that we can get caught up in subconsciously directed stories. We can concoct some up too. If you imagine that your friend doesn't like you and is avoiding you, then you're creating the experience of the shut-out friend. Be mindful of what you create. As a word to the wise, consume television and entertainment mindfully. Curate your entertainment so it enhances the singular universe in which you are the successful multimillionaire.

Would Steve Jobs waste his time eating cheetos all Saturday while watching trash talk shows? I hardly think so. And neither should you.

Principle Number 6: You Are Responsible for Your Experience of Wealth

It's a harsh reality to awaken to the fact that nobody else is responsible for our poverty and lack. In fact, we've designed organizations, charities, and political movements because we believe we are the victims of a villain beyond our control.

As you have read from The Money Formula case studies, nobody is out to get us. We've designed villains in our lives as a means of projecting unresolved situations and emotions. Your husband really isn't a jerk. He's a manifestation of your worst fears. What if you could put down your fears and see him for who he really is: somebody worthy of your love?

I used to have an immense fear of snakes. I used to regularly say, "I hate snakes!" until we had a five-foot-long gopher snake in the backyard of our new miracle house.

I heard my intuition say, "Hate is just an exaggerated fear of something we don't understand."

Once I understood that I was making the snake a scary villain that terrorized my backyard and the safety of my children, I realized that this huge snake was hunting the rats that attracted rattlesnakes. I came to appreciate that this majestic reptile was in fact my friend and faithful servant. And from then on, I never saw a snake in my garden again.

Imagine that the snakes in this metaphor are the enemies we create. The enemy could be the political system, a president, your parents, or even your spouse or children. They are not your enemies. While there are people who *want* to cause harm and want to cause pain and suffering, remember that these people believe in *their* story that you are the villain and they are the saint sent to remove you from their plane of existence.

Without enemies you come to realize that all along you have been manufacturing scenarios and situations to entertain yourself in this backyard we call life. Peter, the bored little boy who sat on the second floor of his bedroom staring out the window, saw an opportunity to entertain himself with stories of the authority figures who were keeping him from having more fun and enjoyment in life. You should have seen the look of bewilderment on his face when he realized he had concocted the story merely as a means of distracting himself from the very conscious business of having fun with life!

It's also equally important that we let go of our expectations of others. We must hold ourselves to our highest ideals and accept others as they are, where they are, and how they are. When it comes to visualizing other people in life, visualize them coming to terms with who they are, and imagine that they will come to realize all the ways they are helping and harming themselves.

It does no good to imagine someone else failing and suffering. When you imagine that failure and suffering, you're just imprinting an image for your subconscious mind to follow. Don't go that route! Instead, imagine them being wiser, kinder, and gentler with themselves and with you!

Principle Number 7: You Are What You Eat

This phrase is passed along so effortlessly in society without much thought. It's a turn of phrase to get people to eat healthier and better so as to not gain weight. But the word eat comes from the Latin *edere*—"to bring forth."

When you attract something, such as bringing forth a spoonful of food to your mouth, with your gravity you are pulling it in. Think about that for a second. Better yet, chew on that.

You have a center of gravity. You are pulling things into yourself. When I designed and taught a personal development course at the INSEEC Business School in France, my Chinese students used to tell me, "You don't get fat with only one spoonful of food."

And in the same way, you don't fill yourself with negativity and attract poverty by accident. You are what you bring forth on a consistent basis.

The Jewish culture has a magical word, often used and misunderstood by the masses, called *abracadabra*. It means, "I will create as I speak." And here, all this time I bet you thought it was some random word a sleight-of-hand illusionist would say to impress his audience with a reappearing bunny. Oh no! In fact, that very act is meant to remind us that we are Great Magicians who call forth our wealth and vitality out of thin air.

The metaphysicians of old considered the air element as the mind. So, if you want to consider "thin air" the mind and "the bunny" our wealth, consider *abracadabra* as your conscious and subconscious acts of pulling wealth to you through the acts of life.

Imagine that you are a beacon of light, like a lighthouse, in the darkness of creation. Whatever light you shine will attract that type of light. Or consider yourself to be a magnet. Whatever type of magnetic force you are, you'll pull like magnetic objects to you. Furthermore, imagine that you're a radio. Whatever station you tune into, you'll receive that frequency.

Whatever it is that you want—in this case great wealth—already exists in your reality. You just have to call it forth. You have to believe that in this reality, the *only* reality, wealth already exists and you are aligning yourself with that wealth. You're consuming only those thoughts, conversations, ideas, and behaviors that attract that wealth to you.

My millionaire clients don't live in a reality of poverty. Just about *all* of my millionaire clients have a story about how they've overcome great obstacles to reach a level of financial success. This is because they had to learn how to let go of poor thinking and climb to the heights of rich thinking. Once again, The Money Formula helps you to let go of poor thinking by eliminating that first poor thought and puts you back on the fast lane of wealth and riches by replacing it with a first thought of wealth.

Once you get that first thought perfected and align it with a powerful feeling of happiness, confidence, faith, and trust, you've set yourself on the path of riches. It's that simple. Really! It is!

There are so many wonderful books out there with advice on how to get rich. They are written by inspired people, who like me, want to see you get rich and be rich. Unfortunately, if you do not correct this first thought—the "original sin" as the Bible calls it—you will doom yourself to a path of poverty.

We often find ourselves on a winding road, wandering aimlessly in the desert like Moses and the Israelites and occasionally finding our way back to the Promised Land. We wander with loose thinking, distracting ourselves with petty drama and entertainment—until the beacon within us says, "Uh-oh, I've wandered too far off course; I've got to be about my Father's business of living abundantly!" Then we scramble temporarily—setting a budget, looking for a job, or networking to get ahead. These temporary things work because we apply our focus and emotions in a short, concentrated burst of energy. They work for that simple reason: we focus our minds and our emotions into a pure thought. But eventually we find ourselves distracted and undisciplined, wondering why we're with money one day and without it the next.

The consistent application of mental and emotional

focus attracts wealth to you. Period. Do you think Warren Buffet wakes up, rolls over to scroll his Facebook feed on his phone to find out what his high school buddy (who he hasn't spoken to in real life in years) is up to? I doubt it. He's up and focused on making more money and planning what he's going to do with it to make even more of it! It's that simple!

People love getting caught up in their stories and the stories of others. It's entertaining and distracting. People want to include you in their stories too!

I sometimes get Facebook messages or text messages from friends I barely know; they'd say, "Oh girl, this happened today. You won't believe what I did and what he said! Isn't that unbelievable?"

They want validation that their stories are real and valid and interesting. People who are focused on their business will not get caught up in petty social drama and distracting stories that pass a lot of time and use up emotional energy. Wealthy people know what is important to them, and they spend all their time, energy, and focus on those priorities.

As a coach, it's easy for me to see what people love by how much time and energy they spend on it. Since you attract what you spend that time and energy on, you're unwittingly saying to the Universe and everyone else on your path that you love it and want more of it.

Look at it this way: wealth is like Lady Justice. She has a blindfold over her eyes and a balance scale in her hands. She does not see what has the most weight (or value and love, in this case) on the balance between wealth and poverty. Thus you get the thing that weighs the most, and wealth will not judge it either way. Wealth is nondiscriminatory; it goes to those who spend their time, energy, and focus cultivating it. Therefore, there are no enemies in life; nobody is keeping you away from money and having a lot of it. Who is in charge of putting the energy on the scales of wealth and poverty? It's not the Lady Wealth. It's you!

So let people fight over power—as if they didn't have it in the first place. Let others brawl for attention—as if they didn't have it in the first place. Let others scheme and fight for wealth and abundance—as if they didn't have it in the first place! None of that is your business. You're in the abundance business, and it's so important that you get to work having it, cultivating it, and expanding your reach.

Be mindful about what you consume—that is, what you attract to yourself. The sheer velocity of what you're attracting will only pull more of it into you. Let others fight like dogs over the scraps, while you see, just outside their view, a banquet placed upon golden plates waiting for you.

Principle Number 8: Love Your Money

As you learned in Principle Number 7, you are a force of nature that attracts that which you are. You are, by nature, a wealthy person. You have all the resources within you to realize and awaken this fact. Unfortunately you've neglected your birthright for too long, seeking pleasure and distraction elsewhere.

Neglect is a powerful, destructive force. Like a castle made of sand on the beach, if you don't spend time protecting your creation from the harsh waves and winds, it will collapse as a consequence of neglect. It will dissolve away, the particles of sand swept somewhere else where it is being called.

Wherever you shift your focus, your reality is being created and solidified for you. Imagine that pristine beach where the sandcastle once was. It has sugary white sand, lush palm trees flush with dates, coconut trees teeming with life, and coral reefs stocked with every kind of delicious fish and seagrass. This is your home of wealth. Everything is already provided for you. It's your . . . Garden of Eden.

You're curious to see what's out there. You want to exercise your imagination, your power, and find out what you can create. So you come up with stories that exist outside of that Garden of Eden. You know, through the faculties of your mind, that you can be in two places at the same time *and* that you attract your creation to yourself.

And *abracadabra*, you find yourself compelled to get on a boat and sail to that place you created in your mind. You go where your mind takes you. You see the horizon of your creation becoming closer and bigger, and at the same time, you turn around and notice that the pristine waters and white sandy beaches are getting smaller . . . until they fade away. Oh, they are still there, but they don't exist in your reality as you get closer and closer to your creative experience; the Garden of Eden becomes just a memory you can't seem to find your way back into. You forgot the way as you focused on getting away.

And that, ladies and gentlemen, is your relationship with money. Go ahead right now and make a list of all of the things you've put before your wealth and abundance. I can tell you some of my distractions from the past. Here goes:

- "Getting" more clients
- "Building" my business
- "Managing" a chaotic home with two small children
- "Dealing" with a husband who constantly traveled for business

These were my stories. These were my distractions. You might say, "Isn't that what you *should* be doing in order to *build* your business?" A lazy thinker would say yes, but in fact, the answer is no.

I created a reality in which I was obsessed with getting more clients—I didn't have enough clients. I *needed* more! I spent years "building" my business when what I needed to focus on was attracting more wealth. Then the elements that would create the foundation and structure of my business would appear at the right juncture.

I used to believe that being a mother was chaotic, so

I created the illusion of being in a hurry, overwhelmed, and having children who were "hard to control." In fact, as Maury Povich says to his guests who take a lie detector test, "*That* was a lie!" I, too, manufactured terrible tots. Once I stopped seeing my children as tough to handle, I began to slow down and enjoy being with them. Now I can't tell you how much FUN it is being a mother!

And finally, I used to believe that in order to have lots of money, I would have to sacrifice time with my husband and share him with the world and his company. I felt that I had to "manage" without him and struggle in his absence. I eventually taught my subconscious self that I can do great without him being home, and when I was ready, I told the Universe that I didn't need my husband to leave town at all for us to have money.

I kid you not, the week before I started writing this book, my husband was slated to go on a business trip. I told myself and the Universe, "Nope. Not happening. He's got to focus on my business next week." He was dumbfounded to hear that his trip was cancelled and someone else was going in his place. I can't tell you how delighted I was to learn this. And, without missing a beat, I thanked the Universe by following through—I named him the CEO of Leslie Inc.

Focus on wealth as if it's your only reality, and it will come. It has to. There literally is no other way—unless you put your focus elsewhere.

Which brings us to our final point in this section: LOVE

your money. Yes, that's right. *Love* your money! It's so important that you do. Here's why:

When you love something, you nourish it. You take care of it. You give it space to grow. You visualize what you'll do with it. You imagine all the places you'll go with it. You imagine it in all its forms, and you love it even more. You respect it. You behave according to its dignity. You speak kindly of it and to it. You create a world in which this thing you love can flourish and you may enjoy it fully.

This can be said for anything: a marriage, a family, children, a car, a home, a garden, and in our case: MONEY!

We have such a bad relationship with money because we've learned not to love it. We've bought in to the false belief that loving money is the root of all evil. Ugh! I'm groaning about how many times I've heard that from clients. How convenient that so many churches tell you not to love money, but they'll gladly take it off your hands so they can love it for you. In fact, they've done a great job of it: as an example the Catholic Church is one of the largest landholders in the world, with just over 177 million acres of property worldwide. If it isn't righteous and holy to be rich, just ask the pope to hold on to your money for you. He'll be happy to do so.

With that said, it is righteous, holy, and good to be exorbitantly wealthy. You require—not need—money to have good teeth, strong bones, and food in your belly. Since you don't have all the time in the world to do everything, your money lets you accomplish what you otherwise could not.

For example, I love gardening. It's actually an understatement when I say I love it. It fills me with joy and pleasure to garden and see my garden flourish. I am so proud when neighbors and passersby stop me in my garden to say, "I've been watching this garden for years, and I want to thank you for making it so beautiful!"

I see my garden as a place of solace and as a source of inspiration for the community. I like to think my garden says to the world, "With patience, attention, and directed focus, you can make a beautiful place for others to see and experience."

I want others to see my garden and think, "Gee, I could do that at home too!" And in my mind, I imagine it improving their property values; together we can collectively raise the whole neighborhood's pride and property values. In other words, I use my garden as a tiny snowflake in an avalanche of community love.

However, I can't always be in my garden to pull every weed and redirect naughty aphids from eating my roses. That's why I hired a trusty gardener named Rafael—my garden angel, I like to call him—to pull weeds, trim trees, and blow leaves. I give him my money to love my garden for me. You see, at every step, there is love, there is intention, and there is an opportunity grow that love. Rafael takes his generous salary home to grow his family and his business. He takes pride in having me as a client. And I have a happy, wonderful garden to share with my family and the community. Everyone wins in this Money Formula.

If you want to love something but can't be there physically for it, don't neglect it; instead give it money by passing that money along to someone else who loves doing what you can't be there to do.

I'll be honest. I don't *love* pulling weeds, but I'll gladly do it if it means that my roses stay aphid-free. And I *love* beautiful roses. Are you beginning to understand where I'm going?

We can't be everywhere all of the time, but we can express our love by creating more of it. Money lets us do just that. There are people who love educating children. I love my children, so I happily pay what could easily amount to a monthly mortgage for a four-bedroom home in a nice neighborhood to ensure that the children I love are educated by people who love to educate them. I feel at peace knowing that my children are being loved in an educational environment. Because I feel at peace, I don't have to waste my mental focus and emotional power wondering if they're safe and happy. I can then turn my focus to what I do best: creating more happiness in the world and getting paid handsomely for it! With my money, I can be in two places at the same time. It's that simple.

You can do this too. There are lots of things you love, and I want you to have more of them all. Maybe not all at once, but as much as your mind can manage so that when you turn your focus to your beautiful garden, it's ready at the exact moment you want to enjoy it. That's the beauty of life!

This is why it is fundamentally important for you to love money. And that very first thought you think when you think of the word *money* sets you on the path of love and abundance. The beautiful thing about money is that it never runs out. Just like life, it's never-ending and abundant. Yes, we'll eventually check out of this life experience through the gateway we call death, but we'll continue on and receive the infinite riches awaiting us on the other side. And then we'll totally experience what used to only exist in our imagination.

To learn more about The Money Formula Principles, log into The Money Formula Academy at http://themoneyformula.leslieinc.org

TEN: LIVING A LIFE OF PURPOSE IS THE SOLUTION FOR WEALTH

The Money Formula is a shortcut for wealth. It's the pathway that cuts away unnecessary suffering, false beliefs, and imaginary situations that perpetuate unprocessed emotional turmoil and loss. The Money Formula is my gift to you so you can get to the trigger of unhealthy and unloving thoughts about money and get back to the business of being alive and fulfilling what you were born to do.

You see, I have a fundamental belief that we are all here on Earth for a specific purpose and that unique purpose exists within us, ready to be born at any minute. Just as a cherry seed is born to create cherries, it can only do so at the right moment and under the correct conditions. The Money Formula helps you correct the conditions and awaken you to your prime directive: to make money!

Consider The Money Formula the means of helping you remember what your special gift to the world is. So many of us misuse our creative force to create a world of havoc, turning others and ultimately ourselves into monsters.

Imagine if Hitler had tapped into his Money Formula. He wouldn't have blamed six million-plus Jews and made them the point of focus in his distorted worldview. What would he have done with that tremendous amount of energy wealth that was available to him? The world will never know.

As I mentioned earlier, to have money, you have to have a purpose for it. You have to have a plan. And that plan falls within your own purpose for living.

A purpose-filled life is essential to maximize health, wealth, and happiness. But you won't know what that is if you don't take the time to love yourself and focus on yourself and your well-being. Don't distract yourself with dramatic stories, non-nutritive television and reading, and unfulfilling work. Remember, money is not the answer. Purpose is the answer.

The greater the purpose you have, the stronger attraction you build for having money. So make your purpose big and powerful, and let it include as many people as possible. When you do, you're using their attractive forces to expand your purpose. That's why people who hire people and create jobs are quick to make millions and billions of dollars. They apply the mental focus of hundreds, if not thousands, of people who are united for a singular purpose.

Singular purpose can be used for good. For instance, Princess Diana helped stop the proliferation of anti-personnel landmines across the globe. She used her personal power, position, and resources to recruit people who wanted to create a safer world for children. Singular purpose can be used for bad too. Hitler didn't slaughter millions of people on his own. He had help, and lots of it. Plus he had tons of money to boot.

The Universe doesn't care or judge as to what is good or bad. It only directs itself according to your purpose, beliefs, thoughts, and emotional energy. A single belief can shape the world, and along with it goes the flow of money.

The Money Formula challenges you to take personal responsibility for your own purposes, beliefs, singular and consistent thoughts, and actions. The Money Formula demands that you hold yourself accountable should you prove yourself to be accountable for so much wealth. Ultimately The Money Formula is a call to action to end your own suffering with a purpose-driven life. Nobody can tell you where to direct your attention. Oh, will they try. That's why there's so many entertaining distractions out there. Those distractions were created so you barely notice the ads in between program breaks directing you where to put your money.

The more money you come to have and the more wealth you build, the more intentional you will find yourself becoming. You won't want to throw your money to the wind. You won't feel the urge to splurge like a lottery winner soon parted with their money. You'll begin to ask yourself, "I have this money, so where do I want it to end up?"

You will be naturally inclined to share your wealth for a good cause. That good cause will then grow your money even more. You'll notice that once you've healed the negative connotation money once had in your life, you'll feel better about it, and you'll be worthy of having more of it. Money won't be a source of power for you anymore. It will be a channel for your own source of power stemming from the creative (mental and emotional) forces within.

Indeed, you'll channel the power within you at higher, more focused levels, and money will follow you. As they say, "A fool and his money are soon parted." *Fool* comes from the Latin word *windbag*. If you've got nothing in your head but air and no purpose, you can quickly kiss any money you attract good-bye.

Like electricity, money is a current. It has to go somewhere. You can attract it to you, but since it's moving and has to keep moving, you'll soon find that without a purpose, it will soon go where it can do the most work.

The Money Formula is the start of your healthy, purposeful journey with money. After you've uprooted the limiting beliefs and negative feelings associated with the word *money*, you'll be free and clear in mind and spirit to appropriate money into purposeful gain. Then you'll read financial advice books with purpose and zeal. You'll make decisions at the grocery store with your end goal in mind. You'll feel stronger at work when negotiating your salary. The Money Formula will change your life because it first started by changing you.

Now that you're aware of the powerful effects of The Money Formula, you're ready to begin this work. You'll never see yourself and your life in the same way again. You'll come to believe and know for certain that this life is a life of abundance. You'll look everywhere around you, and instead of seeing problems and lack, you'll find solutions and abundance.

What's even greater is that you'll start to have better relationships, deeper, more trusting, and more life-affirming. The people who aren't yet ready for the powerful effect of The Money Formula will go their way until their soul and mind is ready for a major life change. Those dramatic people won't bother you anymore. Their magnetic, controlling force will be of no use over you. You'll be in the world, but you won't be of it. You'll be renewed and transformed—and, dare I say, born again.

To learn more about Living A Life of Purpose, log into The Money Formula Academy at http://themoneyformula.leslieinc.org

ELEVEN: THE MONEY FORMULA

As you can see, The Money Formula is quite simple—super simple, VERY simple. It is designed to be simple so you can easily remember the formula for creating abundant wealth. Additionally, once you've used it on yourself, you can teach others how to use The Money Formula too! I want you to help your parents, your cousins, your siblings, your kids, your friends—even your worst enemy. That's right: even those who cause you the greatest amount of pain. They're living in a world of pure imagination that is so chaotic and so painful, they're no longer aware that they're creating it! We've definitely got to help them with The Money Formula. Here's how:

Apply The Money Formula diligently on yourself. Spend a solid three-hour block to focus intensely on your own Money Formula. First, break down all the barriers that stand between you, money, and that happy first thought. Second, neutralize that negative first thought and replace it with a happy one. Additionally, discover all the ways you've created a financial mess in your life: identify the situations, key players, and roles you played for perpetuating your financial suffering. Finally, uncover the essential truths from your experimentation: What were the limiting beliefs? What are the essential truths? What positive affirmation can you apply to this new Money Formula you've created?

When you have done this work on yourself, you will eventually come to see how unfair you've been to your worst enemies. Suddenly they won't seem so bad to you. They won't have an electrical charge over you that controls the direction of your mind and emotional state—and consequently your actions. You will no longer feel a need to be a player in their show of pretend and make believe. You won't drag yourself to their parties and displays for attention. You will then feel compassionate and understanding. You'll identify how much time you've wasted antagonizing them. You'll feel love and forgiveness for them. And finally, you'll let them go to continue on their path of creative play through life.

Remember, I wrote *The Money Formula* because the ten-year-old girl inside of me wanted her parents to be happy. The adult version of me still does. What does the little kid inside of you want for your parents? What could you have done together as a family if you weren't worried for them and if they weren't worried about money? Would you have gone on more family vacations? Had more enjoyable dinners? Read more bedtime stories? Laughed and played more together? While it may be too late for you and me to recapture those opportunities with our parents, you might have kids, and you may realize after having read this far in the book that you're squandering your most precious resource: love.

Your children and the children who haven't yet been born want you to be happy, because if you're happy, they'll learn to make happy associations with money. So, empower your children by empowering yourself! It's never too late to change your relationship with money. And more importantly, it's never too late to change your relationship with yourself and with life.

The Money Formula Step-by-Step

What's the best way to do The Money Formula?
I should mention something about spontaneity. The Money Formula process involves a bit of self-hypnosis. By that, I mean allowing yourself to relax as much as possible and focus on the spontaneous thoughts and feelings that arise. It's like spotting a rare bird. Focus on it, be calm, but don't make a big fuss over what comes up, as the pictures and sensations that come forward are quick to fly away. Your pre-programmed mind will want to jump into thinking what's comfortable, such as what's on TV right now or if you have any Facebook notifications waiting for you.

Be Focused
With that said, focus yourself on getting to the bottom of your Money Formula. Your mental focus is critical at this time. Be sure to follow the steps of The Money Formu-

la to their completion. Yes, if the doorbell rings and you need to answer it, go do that. But come back right away so you can complete the steps with a strong, dedicated train of mind.

Don't Judge and Don't Rationalize

There is a temptation to judge what you see and turn it into a story that justifies why you do something and why others should just deal with it. I want you to do the opposite. I want you to just observe and see where the thoughts and feelings take you.

Additionally, do not try to rationalize your thoughts and feelings if you are working on The Money Formula with a partner—like Albert, who felt self-conscious because he was worried his wife would judge his instincts. Be spontaneous, observant, and accept what comes up intuitively as it comes.

Allow Yourself to Feel

The Money Formula allows you to finally process those unresolved feelings and limiting beliefs. It's your time to remember and feel through the struggle you felt as a child and young person. Allow yourself a moment to grieve, to cry, to feel angry—and then let it pass as you move toward discovering your truth and *the truths* that come forward. It's okay to feel a plethora of emotions. Don't get hung up on them, though; just let them come, say hello, and let them go with appreciation. Those emotions had a job to do, and now that the job is done, they can go back where they came from.

Get Excited

Yes! This is your lucky day! This is the day that you've been waiting for! You get to unload a ton of emotional and mental baggage and exchange it for immeasurable feelings of wealth and abundance. Whoo-hoo! Just think, you manifested me and this book to come into your life at this very moment because you knew someday you would need us. How cool!

Get excited because you are going to turn into someone new, someone wiser, someone more confident. Get ready to be the wealthy and financially confident person that you are meant to be. Your entire life is going to change as a result!

Step 1: Think the Word *Money*

This goes without much explanation: Just think the word *money*.

Allow the very first, immediate thought you think to become emblazoned in the front of your mind.

What did you think?

It could be a word or sets of words. Your first thought could be like Albert's when he saw his parent's tennis court next to their family home. Whatever the thought, immediately write it down and describe it as best as possible.

Step 2: Notice Your First Emotions

Every thought comes with an associated emotion. Every. Single. Thought. There's just no avoiding it.

When I think BMW, I think "baller" and I feel, for a lack of a better word, "Whoo-hoo!"

Notice the emotions that are attached to the word money. Then immediately write down the feeling or set of feelings you emote as a response to that word.

Note: It is critical that you tap into these core emotions. They are the gateway to the key points in your life that cemented these associations.

Step 3: Go to the Earliest Memory of the Emotion

Do you remember how all the *James Bond* movies began? We're staring down the barrel of a gun and then see James Bond walking into view. Imagine walking through that barrel—or being sucked into the emotions . . . similar to Captain Kirk saying, "Beam me up, Scotty!" in *Star Trek*.

When you've gone through the emotions, you'll be transported to the earliest memory when you felt these emotions. Most clients have one principal memory to which the emotions are connected. However, my research has revealed that many have two core memories: usually around the age of ten and around the age of four. If you have a memory that happened at age seven, then so be it. In any case, follow the steps of The Money Formula, just adding another stop along the way to account for the additional memory experience.

Remember to go with the flow and let the experience guide you to the original thought source.

Write down those memories as they appear in your imagination.

Step 4: Examine the Memory

You're going to want to accomplish a few goals in the examination of the memory. Be patient with yourself and practice it in good faith that you will accomplish your goal.

#1 . Notice What Was Happening

At this time, do not do any judging whatsoever. Imagine yourself as a crime scene forensic investigator. You want to go through the scene with as much description and in accurate a sequence as possible. This is why it is essential that you focus on the task at hand.

Comb through the memory for fine details and write them all down. You don't have to write as though you were keeping a journal. Just write down the key facts, like a waitress in a diner taking a short order.

#2. Who Was There?

Part A. It's important to realize who was present in the memory. For many people, it was their parent or parents. If you were not raised by your parents, that's okay—many people weren't. Take stock of all of the actors in the scene.

Part B. Next identify the role each person was playing. The associations should be quick. Don't force them or overanalyze them. You can use words such as *protector*, *bad guy*, and so on. They don't have to be fancy titles.

Part C. What Did They Do? This goes along with their role and doesn't take much analysis or interpretation either. Just allow the spontaneous association to come forward. For instance, in the case of my dad, I noticed that he "reached a limit, felt helpless, and gave up." It's that simple.

Step 5. Identify What Beliefs You Learned
Now ask yourself, "From this experience, what did I learn to believe about life and this word association?"

In my last example, after seeing my dad quit his military career in the Air Force, I discovered the perspective that my dad reached his limits, felt helpless, and gave up. I felt, with that original sense of helplessness, that if I got frustrated with my limits, I would want to quit and would just give up.

Upon observing the sequence of events, these self-sabotaging beliefs will come easily to you. For all of my clients and test subjects, the answers were spontaneous, powerful, and clear.

Remember, at this stage we are learning how limited our perspectives actually were during that experience. We discover limiting beliefs and emotional associations at this stage in The Money Formula. These realizations are not universal truths, but blanket statements to situations in our life that eventually no longer served us. At this point in The Money Formula, it's critical that you move on to the next step.

Step 6: Look for the Patterns in Your Financial Life

This step is critical, because many people have tried to do The Money Formula on their own without accomplishing this important goal. Look for the patterns of the situation you described in Step 4.

Questions to Ask to Reveal Important Patterns

1. When was the most recent time in your life that you noticed similar events from your childhood memories?
2. Who would you say today are playing the key roles from this important memory?
3. What role are you playing this time around as an adult?
4. What emotions do you feel when it comes to your financial life today? Are they similar to this memory?
5. In what way are present events and habitual patterns rooted in this memory?
6. What has the limiting belief(s) in Step 5 taught you to believe about life/God/the Universe by way of characteristics (unfair, unloving, selfish, etc)?
7. What did you learn about yourself at this time?

These questions will help you flesh out the overarching patterns that your old Money Formula has created in your life in this present day. You can get creative and come up with your own questions, although rest assured that the most important patterns will be most obvious and intuitive to notice.

Step 7. Uncover Your New Truths

You will now begin to look at ways to neutralize the old emotion and word connection. You will also be able to replace the old connection with a positive new thought and emotion.

Note that this step in The Money Formula immediately follows Step 6, and in many cases, it includes Step 6.

Answer These Questions to Reveal New Beliefs:

1. What role do you no longer need to play when it comes to money?
2. Who were you making out to be the bad guy in this story?
3. What characteristics were you giving others to create a sense of drama?
4. What is possible for you now that you know you don't need to do/feel/act that way anymore?
5. What was your old Money Formula, and what is your new Money Formula?
6. Money used to = X, but now Money, when you think of it, equals _____.

7. You used to feel this way about money, but now you feel _____ (joy, happiness, calm, confidence).

You'll discover, for example, "Wow! I realized that all this time I needed permission to get money. I don't need permission anymore. I can just say to myself, 'You need more money, so go ahead and have it!'"

You may also say, "For so many years, I've played the victim in my financial life. I don't need to run away from creditors and make them look like they're loan sharks! I've got the loan, and I'm going to pay it off because I can, and I don't have to distract myself anymore with this story of being a victim who can't pay their bills!"

In this step, you will have successfully created your brand-new Money Formula. This means that you're able to take control of what you think and how you feel about the word *money*—and every other word in the financial dictionary.

To get The Money Formula Worksheet, log into The Money Formula Academy at http://themoneyformula.leslieinc.org

TWELVE: APPLYING THE MONEY FORMULA

Keep The Money Formula Simple

The first time for everyone usually takes about fifteen minutes. Be mindful not to get too convoluted in your steps. I've noticed that if you go on a tangent, it can be difficult to find your way back if you're not going through the process with an expert.

Stay focused on the seven steps, and keep your answers simple. Remember, this process is designed to be simple, quick, and effective. Don't make it, like your old financial life, complicated!

Have Fun and Share

Have fun with the process and revel in the discovery of all those old beliefs and habits that no longer have a grip on your life and finances. Share your discovery with your close friends and family members. Tell them just how much better you feel—and how they can feel better too. Your family will be amazed to learn how they were right about you being dramatic all along. Just kidding! Although I'm sure they'll be grateful to know that your judgments about them have disappeared.

Keep Applying The Money Formula

You will find, my friend, that there are roots upon roots of limiting beliefs and attitudes that are attached to your first thoughts of money and everything associated with money. I encourage you to go down the rabbit hole even further, unlocking every negative association you've ever made with money and the financial world.

Here is a list of words I recommend you apply The Money Formula to:

Bills

Creditors

Financing

Debt

Mortgage

Car payment

Utility Bills

Business

Bankruptcy

Divorce

Alimony

Separation

Judgment

Vacation

Relaxation

Bonus

Time Off

Sick Leave

Workers' Compensation

Credit cards

Job

Work

Bank account

Financial crisis

Creditor

To download a financial vocabulary, log into The Money Formula Academy at http://themoneyformula.leslieinc.org

This is just a list of words most people use when they talk about money. The whole point of using The Money Formula is that you feel confident about the entire dictionary of financial terms. We don't just want you to be financially literate—we want you to feel GOOD and HAPPY every time you think, read, and speak these words.

You see, if you're not intimidated by financial terms, you're going to feel good about going to a car dealership and discussing the financing of your new car. You're going to feel confident when you go in for a salary negotiation. You're going to feel good when shopping for a home mortgage. Better yet, you're going to feel good about having the MONEY to pay for all of it!

Feeling good about money takes the power out of other people's hands. When you don't feel afraid about making your mortgage payment, or stressed about sending your children to school, or anxious about going on a paid vacation, you won't ever allow anyone to manipulate you into believing you don't deserve the good stuff life has to offer.

Additionally, nothing will seem so far out of reach for you. Go on an exotic vacation? Why not? Open a business that creates immense value in the world? Why not? Create a product that will save lives? Sure! Write a play that will change the way people see society? Go for it!

The Money Formula will give you the added self-confidence to achieve anything you want in life because you know two important facts:

- There are no barriers to your success.
- There are no enemies standing in your way.

When you are fully aware of these two important facts, you will be unstoppable and unlimited. You will go for your dreams. You will be your truest self. You will speak honestly and from the heart. You will be the very best version of yourself. I don't even have to guarantee it because I know for sure you'll never go back after applying The Money Formula to your life.

Now that you are able to get to the source of the resistance in your financial life, you can easily and fluidly move through it. Life is not so much a battle, but instead it's a wonderful act of creation. You'll be so curious about what you can create that everything that once served as a distraction will not seem so interesting anymore. Before you know it, your life will be an experiment in Pure Thought.

I want you to know that The Money Formula changed my life for the better because it empowered me to change myself—or rather, what I thought I was and who I thought I was. I now realize that I am not the little girl standing on the soggy grass on Solomon Street. Instead, I am a powerful, creative force that harnesses the power of Pure Thought to experience this reality. I know it all sounds so sci-fi or spiritual, but applying The Money Formula in some ways feels like a religious experience, in that I'm transformed, healed, and renewed.

As I write this, I imagine that you will feel the exact same way—or maybe even better! I imagine that you'll go through similar experiences as you come to terms with all that you have allowed to limit you and keep you down for so long. I'm so glad that you're ready now to apply The Money Formula, talk about it, and share it with the world. Because this day begins the first day of the rest of your life as a wealthy, rich, and powerful individual.

I look forward to hearing your stories, to meeting you,

and to knowing just how exactly The Money Formula transformed your life, personal finances, and business. I want to know what steps you took *after* applying The Money Formula to increase your bounty. I'm ready. Are you?

To take the next steps in applying your Money Formula, log into The Money Formula Academy at http://themoneyformula.leslieinc.org

THIRTEEN: THE POWER OF GRATITUDE

Gratitude deserves its own separate chapter because gratitude is what binds all of this and The Money Formula together. It's the tie that binds us in the love of money and our relationship with it. Gratitude is what allows our conscious mind to say, "Well done for what you've created!"

Gratitude is a moment when we are conscious of our mind saying, "I'm alive, I'm a creator, and this is exactly what I created with my pure thought!"

The next time you find yourself in a situation that you're not really in love with, say to yourself, "Thanks for creating this situation, and I know I can do better. What thought and feeling combination can I change to improve upon this?"

It's so important to thank yourself and others for being a part of your creative experience. It's especially important to thank the Universe for giving you exactly what you need at all times—nothing more, nothing less. The wonderful thing about gratitude is that it's empowering and freeing. It allows you to say, "I can do something with this situation. I have everything I need!"

In so many ways, we're like MacGyver when we're in a state of gratitude: we can realize our creative faculties to make something out of any situation. You can make it worse with your thinking, or you can make it infinitely better! The choice is truly yours.

With gratitude, I'm led to remind you of the power of grace. Grace lets you stand back and say, "Hmm . . . that didn't happen exactly as I'd like. What doubts or limitations did I have in me that allowed this to happen?"

Grace is our ultimate gift for fixing impure thinking and feeling. If we realize in a moment of gratitude that we've created a mess, we can stop that train of thought before it hits the bottom, and we can think again! We can forgive ourselves for our wrong thinking and false feeling and start over.

I'd like to think that The Money Formula is an act of grace. It's a way of saying, "I stunk up my financial situation quite badly, but I can turn it around starting right now with this fresh thought."

Gratitude is the attitude that can keep the good stuff coming, and grace is the attitude to change course whenever we find ourselves offtrack. There's plenty more of the good stuff and the bad stuff, and gratitude and grace reminds us of this very important fact! So, choose wisely and know that it's never too late to make a course correction.

To listen to me talk about gratitude, log into The Money Formula Academy at http://themoneyformula.leslieinc.org

FOURTEEN: LIVING A NEW FINANCIAL LIFE

You are now living a new financial life whether or not you consciously recognize it. You've taken the first steps, and through the application of The Money Formula, you now realize that you don't have to be a financial whiz with an MBA or PhD in statistics. Nor do you have to be a business titan in order to have a lot of cash and feel good about your net worth.

I want you to remember that you don't have to *know* how things are going to work out. You just have to change your relationship with whatever it is you think of. As long as you think wealth and feel equally good about it, the path of unfolding will reveal itself so that your journey is assuredly a good one.

The Universe is on your side. It works faithfully for you day and night, even while you're sleeping. Why can't money? Michael Jordan makes more money in his sleep than most people do their entire lives. Do you think he's got a great relationship with money? You bet he does!

You don't have to equate your net worth to your self-worth. You don't have to equate your financial future with your financial past. And you don't have to live the financial life of your parents, or their parents too! You are truly free to create for yourself whatever makes you most happy. Because, when you're happy, the world suddenly feels so much richer. And that's the kind of world I want to live in for sure.

To share your testimonial experience using The Money Formula, log into The Money Formula Academy at http://themoneyformula.leslieinc.org

ACKNOWLEDGMENTS

I want to thank my parents for being the vessels that brought me through to this side of creation. I want to thank my aunts, especially Auntie Fe, for being such strong women. Thanks to them and my mom, I've associated the word *woman* with boundless strength, humor, and enthusiasm. I feel good being a woman and for being me, and I want to thank you for this feeling.

I want to thank my dad and his parents, my grandparents. Thanks to them, I went on this journey in the exploration of financial freedom. Because of you, I am indeed financially free. Thank you.

I want to thank the Habitat For Humanity, Ms. Vicky Kissinger Loehr, the University of North Florida, and the countless other charitable organizations that invested in me. With every dollar and piece of advice you gave me, I made sure to make use of it and pay it forward. Thank you.

A special thanks to my French family for bringing me Franck and my children, Donavon and Harper. What precious gifts! Thank you for your generosity and total and complete acceptance. With you, I learned the value of family.

To my Leslie Inc. team: Franck, Ana, Josh—without you this book would have never happened. Thanks for the good ideas! They always take us to fun places. I love our team and Leslie Inc. wouldn't be possible without you.

www.ingramcontent.com/pod-product-compliance
Lightning Source LLC
Chambersburg PA
CBHW071718210326
41597CB00017B/2528